THE SHAMAN'S VISION

Earl F. Walborg
(Lone Hawk)

The Shaman's Vision
Copyright 1996

Cover art by Bear Romero

Medicine Bear Publishing Company
216 Paseo del Pueblo Norte
Taos, N.M. 87571

ISBN 0-9651546-6-1
Library of Congress CCN 96-078431

Dedication

To those ancestors who sought and gained insight
through wonder, ordeal, terror, or pain,
Whose images of non-material reality still lurk
within my brain,
To my wife and family whose love, care and
understanding nurtured reflection,
And to those progeny of bloodline and spirit who
prayerfully seek direction.

Author's Preface

I never cease to wonder at the way the vision entered my conscious thought. In retrospect, I can discern numerous life experiences that heightened my receptivity to the vision, but it was the events of Thanksgiving Day in 1987 that opened my mind's eye to the intruding mystical scenes that are revealed in the following pages. Thanksgiving has always been a joyous occasion for our family; a time for the gathered generations to relate recent happenings, reminisce about our shared past, enjoy the fellowship of lengthy, boisterous, tasty meals and express gratitude to our common Creator.

In a tradition established over the decade prior to 1987, my sons and I arose early on Thanksgiving Day to hunt deer on acreage we own a short distance north of our home. For me, hunting is not a sport, but rather participation in a primal ritual instituted by our hunter-gatherer forebears, a ritual largely lost or perverted by a technological society dissociated from the land and Nature. In the hunt, I become one with Nature and utter the ancient prayer for nourishment: *"May my animal and plant neighbors allow their flesh and seed to sustain m e and my family today, knowing that tomorrow m y body will nourish the progeny of those I slay."* Hunt or harvest, honorably and humbly performed, is a portal to the profound understanding that physically and spiritualy we are participants in a creative cycle of eternal life.

That Thanksgiving, I chose to hunt from a tree-stand rudely constructed between two upraised arms of a postoak tree whose trunk divided close to the ground. In the pre-dawn darkness, I climbed up to the platform and pulled up the rope to which my rifle was tied and settled in for the wait. Although we have killed deer before on our land, it's not prime deer country and I was assured abundant and welcome time for meditation. Being particularly fond of the breaking dawn, I watched trees, shrubs and grasses slowly materialize like a sharpening apparition...the way mystical insights would soon steal into my mind. Although the sun had not yet peered over the horizon, daybreak was announced by a chorus of raucous crows.

The black winged messengers of the unknown also announced an unexpected arrival. I was suddenly aware of a pulse of fear rushing through my body as a gripping tightness intensified beneath my breastbone. As my limbs began to weaken, I tried to stay focused and clear to the impending reality. Although I had experienced no prior heart problems and was in reasonably good physical condition for a 52-year- old male, I knew that a heart attack was a real possibility. I mustered the strength to descend from the tree-stand and call to my eldest son who was hunting a short distance away. He immediately drove his pale and weakened father to the local rural hospital. That morning was the beginning of several long days and nights spent lying on my back looking up...looking up from an emergency room table, looking up at the ceiling of an ambulance during transport to a regional hospital, looking up in an operating room just before coronary artery by-pass surgery, looking up in a recovery room full of tubes and wires and finally looking up in a hospital

room clutching a pillow tightly to my aching chest. During those days, I learned much about the fragility and finite nature of material life and much about the love of family. At the mercy of others and our Creator, I learned that mystical insights are more easily apprehended when personal identity is at peril and physical security is departing. Under the spell of a Creator and Destroyer, never before known so intimately, I was blessed with the vision that unfolds on the following pages.

I look back in deep gratitude to that Thanksgiving Day when I was suspended between earth and heaven in the upraised arms of a postoak tree.

Earl F. Walborg

'Lone Hawk'

August, 1996

The Shaman

The drum-entranced shaman becomes enveloped
in the night-chilled mist,
Securely fastened to the earth where echoes from
the past persist,
Stationed beneath the stardust path, that sure sign
of a plan imposed,
Seized by message-filled visions from without, yet
from within disclosed.

At Yggdrasil's foot the shaman dips clear water
from Mimir's well,
Communes with ancestors and sees visions that
the future foretell.
Like Odin, he comprehends that wisdom comes
only at great cost,
And that profound insights are attained when
security is lost.

With wisdom and strength, gained from an in-
tensely personal ordeal,
He rejects belief coercion, preferring to care,
teach and heal.
The shaman feels the uniqueness of his
spiritual journey
And understands the entry can be unlocked by
more than one key.

THE SHAMAN'S VISION

Within a still and dark abyss the EagleDove
stretches its strong, enfolding wings;
And issuing from deep inside its beating breast,
a cooing peaceful song it sings.
Wing-driven wind and morning song spread
outward in a forever expanding sphere.
Though mingling in myriad ways, the primal note
of each windsong is there to hear.

Amid the growing, churning turbulence of twirl-
ing, whirling, spinning winds and songs,
Melodious windsongs are flinging into space and
time, where and whence each belongs.
Mid ripples begetting ripples and eddies begetting
eddies, the heavens form,
While rush of wind and lilt of song blend to create
harmony within the storm.

Wings unfurl and with a mighty lurch the Awesome Bird flies outward to soar afar.
Eagle eyes search the vast expanse for a swirling
windsong dreaming to be a star.
Once spied, talons capture the turbulence and a
sharp beak rends it in two,
Flinging a cool light into the nighttime darkness
and a warm light into the blue.

Swooping upon a fleeing windsong, the EagleDove
continues its selection.
Movement is arrested and transmuted to a sparkle
that imparts direction.
Then the sparkling one bursts asunder, embers into
the far reaches are dispersed,
A chorus of twinkling lights encircling the
stationary one that sparkled first.

Swept by the winds of the EagleDove's wings,
cosmic lights congregate in a wide band,
That dusty path in the night sky, evidence against
the random and for the planned.
Returning to its central perch, the Awesome Bird
pronounces the heavens complete,
A magnificent choir of whirling windsongs
synchronized to the Eagle's heartbeat.

* * * *

Despite the wonders of the realm, loneliness stirred
within the Eagle and the Dove;
Then from united yearnings there appeared a fertile
egg, conceived in joy and love,
A beautiful sphere, painted hues of blue and green
and overlaid by wisps of white,
Incubated in the warm light's garden, but ever
within the Dove's watchful sight.

Bathed in penetrating warmth, the egg commences
to hatch in mysterious ways.
Amid spurts of fire and cataclysmic tremors, land
breaks through a watery haze;
Forming mountains, valleys and canyons; creating
rivers and isolating lakes.
Warming waters effervesce into ebony clouds as
rolling thunder awakes.

The Eagle's eerie screech turns to lightning and into
a thunderstorm disappears.
Within the ozone new forms emerge and descend
on sea and earth like happy tears.
Each tear begetting unique, reproducing shapes and
forms in tints of brown and green,
Each tearform evolving and spreading as directed
by the Great Feathered Unseen.

A second screech turned lightning bolt strikes a
secluded bay where destined forms reside.
In heated waters old forms acquire scales and fins to
course the oceans far and wide.
With yet another screech-lightning fish gills trans-
form to lungs, and legs arise from fins.
As walking forms disperse to the wet and damp and
dry, a new adventure begins.

Soft cooing emanates from the ever watchful Dove
and falls upon her hatchlings.
Her lonesome voice, heard only by destined walking forms, transmutes legs to arms and wings.
Those possessing wings intrude into the heavens as
if searching for the Great Above,
Those with arms embrace as if to mimic the
enfolding wings of the EagleDove.

The Eagle and the Dove each pluck seven perfecting
feathers from the other's breast,
And let them flit and flutter downward upon four
upraised arms waiting to be blessed.
They settle on the destined pair, seven on the one
and seven on the other,
Selecting the first to become the father and the
second to be the mother.

Two Eagle feathers and one from the Dove fly like
arrows into the father's heart,
Livening feather-arrows from the Great Above,
spirits unwilling to depart.
A primal message is delivered as feather-spirits
penetrate flesh and bone:
"Dependence rightly placed is the most precious
jewel, the brightest that has ever shown."

Three Eagle feathers and one from the Dove
penetrate his ears and enter his brain.
The feathers intermingle and tickle his mind, while
singing that ancient refrain:
"Remember the EagleDove, your Father and
Mother, and the wonders they have wrought,
For life's wonders are the EagleDove's gifts, bless-
ings that can never be earned or bought."

Three Dove feathers and one from the Eagle impale
like sharpened spears the mother's heart,
Energizing feather-spears from the First Mother,
love-spirits that never depart.
Primeval words are softly whispered as the feather-
spirits pierce her naked breast:
"Like the EagleDove, nuture all creation in love, for
through you...all will be blessed."

Two Dove feathers and one from the Eagle enter
her ears and permeate her mind,
Reciting in perfect harmony that age-old message
worth more than gold refined:
"Remember the EagleDove, your Mother and
Father, and the wonders they have wrought,
For life's wonders are the EagleDove's gifts, blessing
that can never be earned or bought."

Spirit names bestowed on the feather-pierced pair
are Eagle Feather and Cooing Dove.
Happily embracing, they meld together in a
beautiful oneness of love.
In oneness they feel a gentle breeze stirred by the
flutter of the EagleDove's wing,
And hear the promise: "Through your progeny
the breastfeathers will continue to sing."

As new worlds reverberate in their skulls, eyes
search the heavens in awe and wonder.
Again, clouds darken and screech-lightning dances
to earth, announced by the drum of thunder.
In a pall of smoke, dancing screech-lightning etches
a poem on a canyon wall,
A one verse blessing from the EagleDove, written
to enlighten and to enthrall.

"The egg and its hatchlings are your garden, yours
to use, to nurture and to protect.
The EagleDove's creative power and love are yours
to enjoy and to reflect.
Freedom to be and to do proceeds from the
EagleDove's parental affection,
An enfolding affection that gladly provides more
direction that protection. "

From the oneness of the chosen pair children come
to the garden to work and play.
Each child hears replicate breastfeathers plead,
saying: "Take me, remember and obey."
The children are led into the sacred canyon and
shown the poem on its wall;
Then each admonished that it holds the secret to
true happiness and standing tall.

The first family heard the breastfeathers at each
rising and setting of the sun.
They wore a path to the sacred wall and gave
thanks for what the EagleDove has done.
Loving care abounded, food and shelter arrived as
presents from a happy earth;
Life was danced in mirth, with creative daily labor
providing fulfilling worth.

One day a buzzard circled over the canyon, casting
down its shadowy pall.
It chanced to pass over Eagle Feather as he
contemplated the sacred wall.
Within the dark shadow he knew this adventure is
to an interval confined.
Gracious affection must be reflected before the Black
Priest has dined.

Years later the buzzard's shadow settled on Eagle
Feather as he breathed his last.
Circled round the corpse, his bloodline clan realized
the sureness of present and past.
In awe they witnessed the breastfeathers of the
EagleDove exit his skull and chest,
And a whirlwind that carried each breastfeather to
the sky in a churning tempest.

The buzzard descended on Eagle Feather's belly,
tearing flesh from limb and chest,
Dining not as the hated enemy, but like a
welcome and expected guest.
Shifting to Eaglefeather's blood-stained breast, the
Black Priest quickly snatched out each glazed eye,
Then clutching the eyes in his talons, he chased the
breastfeathers upward to the sky.

As the breastfeathers circled high, his clan sensed it
was Eagle Feather's parting dance.
With great sadness they carried his lifeless body to
the sacred canyon's entrance.
Heeding his wish, into each sensing orifice of his
skull they placed an acorn,
And planted him upright in the sod, facing east
toward the sunrise of each new morn.

Eagle Feather's seven acorns sprouted to mark the
entrance to the sacred wall,
Becoming seven oaks, a symbol of the Black Priest's
message to the children all:
"Life is bounded by four corners and to intervals of
future, present and past;
Life in the finite is lived in the shadow of the
Infinite, the First and Last."

As the years passed the descendant's eardrums
slowly deafened to the breastfeather's call;
And vines and ferns were allowed to obscure the
poem on the sacred canyon wall.
Harmony ceased when the progeny chose
independence from the Father and Mother;
Then the verdant garden was plundered and in
anger brother turned against brother.

Tears flowed as the Great Unseen watched the
progeny of Eagle Feather lose their way.
The Eagle wished to end this misadventure in a
consuming lightning display;
But the Dove plucked an Eagle wingfeather and let
it fall like a fragile flower,
In hope that one of the descendants would catch its
message and uplifting power.

The wingfeather came to rest on an outcast who
had fallen on his face to pray.
Accepting the wingfeather, he opened the over-
grown path to the light of day;
Then with the aid of innocent children the poem
was uncovered for all to see.
Each stood silent in the poem's spell, once again
discerning the breastfeather's plea.

But joy above was short-lived for again the progeny
became blind to the path.
Again and again the Eagle thought of unleashing
his lightning in fiery wrath,
But again and again the Dove sent wingfeathers to
the outcasts kneeling below;
And again and again the EagleDove its mercy and
forgiveness did bestow.

Some who accepted wingfeathers were ridiculed,
some killed by lance or knife or stone.
Even the Dove was angered by the deeds she was
resigned to accept, but not condone.
Finally, in exasperation she said, "I myself will
go to show the way.
Surely, that will convince our wayward creation
and usher in a bright new day."

In a wrenching, groaning shudder the Dove
separates from the Eagle and flies free.
Her lofty aerie forsaken, she spirals downward on
her mission of mercy,
A risky act, a vicarious interpretation of words
etched on a wall,
A caring participation, lending voice to the
breastfeather's primeval call.

* *   * *   * *

Hidden under fallen leaves of the seven oaks, an
orphaned infant cries in fright,
Unaware that his parents lay dead, slain by six
thieves under the cover of night.
The last act on their way to the sacred wall was to
hide the only wealth they knew,
A hope that the clouds would part and the progeny
would again gaze into the blue.

Dawn's dew-tears fall from the branches above onto
the infant suffering below.
Then down the sacred path a lowly woman comes
to pray in the sun's early glow.
Alerted by the moan of wind through the oaks, her
eyes fall upon the bloody deed.
Bending down, she hears dry dead leaves utter the
pleading whimpers of a child in need.

Brushing the leaves away, she discovers the baby
boy shivering in the cold.
She warms the child against her breast, oblivious to
the dance about to unfold.
A happy breeze whistles through the branches,
bestowing a new name on the woman.
Feather Bearer was about to become a dancer in a
grand and ancient plan.

When night fell again, the Dove entered the boy-
child nursing at Feather Bearer's breast.
The new mother perceived a penetrating warmth
and sensed she had been strangely blest.
Looking down, the dim moonlight revealed two
wingfeathers clutched tightly in his small hand;
One wingfeather from an Eagle and one from a
Dove, a love-sign long ago planned.

The sign was graciously acknowledged and Two
Wingfeathers became the boy-child's name,
A symbol of the EagleDove's faithful care, an
omen of an aim to reclaim.
As the boy-child grew, Feather Bearer pondered the
mystery that had been conceived.
A gift for all the children of Eagle Feather and
Cooing Dove had been received.

As a young lad, Two Wingfeathers often gazed
upon the poem that held life's key.
As a young man, he fasted in the sacred canyon and
heard the breastfeather's plea.
In a dream-like trance he felt the Eagle whisper,
"Find the wayward and heal their pain,
Live the primal message, recite the sacred poem
and chant the ancient refrain."

With purpose Two Wingfeathers walked to the
four corners, visiting each tribe and clan.
Joyfully, he danced to the Unseen Drum, following
the beat of an ancient plan.
Many from different tribes and clans joined
together, dancing in expanding rings;
And as they danced, they perceived the rhythym,
the beating of the Eagle's mighty wings.

His teachings were plain and clear, "First, revere
the EagleDove, your Father and Mother;
Second, be a servant to the progeny, for each is your
sister or brother;
Third, protect and utilize with care the beautiful
blue-green egg and its hatchlings;
Believe and live these teachings and you will dance
in rhythm with the EagleDove's wings."

Not all joined the spirited dancers, fearing their
loss of control over others.
Proud chiefs and pious priests and men who had
received more possessions than their brothers,
Conspired with the undiscerning to seize the
Leader and end the disruptive dance.
The conspirators had seen the first flower of spring,
but could not smell its fragrance.

At the year's first full moon the circle dancers gath-
ered inside the sacred canyon,
Awaiting the arrival of Two WingFeathers after
the setting of the sun.
The drums began a festive beat, anticipating the
Dance of the Spring Flowers,
A dance to acknowledge and experience the
EagleDove's reviving powers.

Meanwhile, six conspirators planned to end the
dance and assure their own survival.
Beneath the seven oaks they silently awaited
the Dance Leader's arrival.
Gripping tightly in their fists gnarled clubs fashioned from boughs of the mighty sacred oaks,
They convinced themselves it was their duty to
expose Two Wingfeathers as a hoax.

Alone in the twilight Two WingFeathers walked
quietly along the sacred path.
As he passed by the oaks, the plotters sprang from
the shadows to vent their pent-up wrath.
Clubs fell in succession and Two Wingfeathers fell,
long-bones broken, his blood spilling.
At the breaking of his skull there sounded the
awful crack of nearby screech-lightning.

Frightened by the screech-lightning, the conspira-
tors sought to conceal their bloody act,
Covering the crumpled body beneath an altar
fashioned from rocks neatly stacked.
Under the pressure of the heavy stones the Dance
Leader exhaled his final breath,
While smoke from fresh cedar boughs and gnarled
oak clubs mingled to hide the odor of death.

At the canyon circle-dancers waited as the full
moon rose higher in its track;
Then a shadow slowly extinguished its light till the
canyon became deathly black.
In eerie darkness the anxious dancers sensed the
powers of evil had prevailed,
The Dove's ultimate love-sign had been rejected,
the grand and ancient plan had failed.

Then in silent fear the dancers intently watched the
    evil shadow crawl away.
Just at regained fullness the Dance Leader appeared
        and the circle began to sway.
The drum cadence quickened as dancers realized
    Two Wingfeathers was really there.
Arms and bodies gyrated in joyful frenzy as
    thanksgiving replaced dispair.

The circle-dancers' fervor swelled as fading moon-
        light yeilded to dawn's amber glow.
Profuse rivulets of sweat flowed from undulating
        bodies moving to and fro.
Then, as an approving sign, a cool morning
    rainshower fell from a cloudless sky.
Rain and sweat mixed to form a muddy ooze,
    rescuing an earth that was parched and dry.

Dawn's light revealed Two Wingfeathers sweating
blood while he danced to the ancient refrain;
And where blood touched muddy ooze flowers
grew, evidence of the egg's rebirth through pain.
Soon the ground was a blanket of fragrant spring
flowers in every hue and shade.
The dancers then understood that the EagleDove's
power and love had been displayed.

Footprints of the circle-dancers disappeared before
drying in the warming sun.
Only bloodstained footprints were baked in place, a
memory of what the Dove has done.
To this day the bloodstained footprints remain on
the canyon floor for all to behold,
An urgent reminder that the story of Two
Wingfeathers must not go untold.

The dancing continued at fervor pace even as
another moon rose and fell.
Each circle-dancer felt the EagleDove's heartbeat
and swayed to its engaging spell.
Though feet moved over the fragrant carpet,
strangely flowers neither withered nor died.
Upon inhaling the sweet aromas, strength to ex-
hausted muscles was supplied.

As the moon stoops to caress the earth, Two Wingfeathers turns and the dancers follow.
Approaching the canyon portal, the Leader acquires
a blinding radiant glow;
And at the precise moment the moon becomes
enveloped in the earth's warm caress,
The sun-like radiance disappears beneath the altar
stones that crushed him lifeless.

Motionless, dancers stand stunned in disbelief as
dawn pierces through the eastern sky.
In fear the six altar builders shudder to the ground,
uttering an anguished cry.
First rays from a fire-orange sun strike as swift as
lightning upon the altar stones.
Purifying heat turns stones to dust, revealing
fragile, broken avian bones.

The conspirators wail and writhe upon the bone-
dry earth; their heinous deed exposed.
Truth dawns with awful force; their hard hearts to
freely offered breastfeathers had been closed.
Slowly each writhing body shrinks, metamor-
phosing into a squirming maggot;
Each consigning itself to feed upon feather-
fled bodies as they waste and rot.

A searching, lonesome screech of the Eagle
penetrated the languid morning air.
Bone and feather reassembled, a sign that
brokenness is not beyond repair.
Before awestruck dancers there fluttered forth a
radiantly beautiful white Dove.
Speckled with crimson, a sign of the Awesome
Bird's eternal and unfailing love.

The Speckled Dove circled low over the dancers
as if bestowing a blessing.
Then, in reply to a second lonesome screech, the
Dove began heavenward climbing,
Until at last the white radiance disappeared
into the enveloping blue.
A third screech, not lonesome, pronounced the
love-sign completed by the Great One in Two.

Shadowed by the mighty oaks, the dancers fall
entranced in thankful contemplation,
Slowly understanding EagleDove's risky
act of caring participation.
The engaging life of Two Wingfeathers is the
source for constant emulation.
Only rejecting the First Spring Flower begets
the maggots of separation.

As the sun meets the earth, swaying elation
replaced thankful contemplation.
Then, in response to the Heartbeat Above, dancers
quicken in wild celebration.
In the moon-absent darkness light streams earth-
ward from an embrightened wide starry band,
That ancient sparkling pathway, sure evidence
against the random and for the planned.

As dawn pierces through the darkness, distant and
contented cooing of the Dove is heard.
Recognizing that Two Wingfeathers had departed,
a deep heart-felt loss recurred.
Was the progeny really left alone, with only
distant cooing to inspire?
Who would enliven the ancient words? Who
would lead the circle dance and chanting choir?

Minds and bodies spent, dancers departed the
canyon in mixed wonder and despair.
Passing the sacred trees, each plucked two oak
leaves, a remembrance of the Eagle's care.
Imprinted into tightly clenched fists, the leaves
grew warm; then, like white-hot embers, burned.
To assuage the pain fists opened, revealing not
leaves but Two Wingfeathers returned.

With thankful upraised arms the progeny understood they had not been left alone.
Wingfeathers still spiral downward, bearing words
and power from the Unknown Yet Known.
Reaching the high plain above, the dancers gazed
back upon a sunlit rainshower,
Adorned with a brilliant arc of colors, a
promise-bow from the First Spring Flower.

* * * * * *

Visit the sacred canyon often, meditate on its
primal one-verse blessing,
Sing and dance to the ancient refrain, enjoy all
the flowered aromas of spring,
Gaze upon footprints of the Speckled Dove, and
recall broken avian bones resurrecting,
Remember the sacred mott, for its leaves still warm
hand and heart at each offering.

Even now the mighty oaks still beckon the progeny
to enter their cool shade;
In quiet solitude to hear dew-tears fall, to quake
in awe, yet kneel unafraid;
To listen as the Dove's cooing wind-song whispers
through tender leaves and sturdy boughs;
To let a distant screech impale your heart and
welcome the true wisdom it endows.

Lone Hawk

About the Author

Influenced by 22 years in academic science and over 50 years of participation in traditional Protestant Christianity, the author has been a reluctant mystic, only recently propelled along that path by wonder, curiosity, coincidence and the shadow of death. During a career transition in the mid '80s, he kept a journal; and it was then that he first began to put his thoughts into verse. Also during that period, family and business took him to Guatemala where he became intrigued with Native American religious thought. This further deepened his awakening and he realized the need for a renewed spirituality and ethic that flows from unique personal encounters with the Creator. The Shaman's Vision resulted from one such encounter. The author and his wife live in Smithville, Texas and Antigua, Guatemala.